# Neuschwanstein Castle

Official guide

Revised by
Uwe Gerd Schatz
and
Friederike Ulrichs

Bayerische
Schlösserverwaltung

# Contents

*Following pages: Upper Courtyard: on the left is the Palas, on the right the Connecting Building with the Knights' House in the middle; the windows are in the Romanesque style.*

*One of three majolica swans made for Neuschwanstein Castle by Villeroy & Boch, 1884. The body is hollow and was used as a container for plants and flowers.*

*Design for the window arcades on the first floor of the Knights' House by the scene painter Christian Jank, 1870, with naturalistic plants and animals from a programme by Hyazinth Holland; the trees are representations of the World Ash Tree Yggdrasil, the roots of which were home to the dwarf-like Nibelungen.*

# »Idea«

Ludwig II announced his plan to build »New Hohenschwangau Castle«, which was only called »Neuschwanstein« after his death, in the following letter dated 13 May 1868 to his friend Richard Wagner: »It is my intention to rebuild the old castle ruin of Hohenschwangau near the Pöllat Gorge in the authentic style of the old German knights' castles ... The location is one of the most beautiful one could find, holy and unapproachable, a worthy temple for the divine friend who has brought salvation and true blessing to the world. It will also remind you of Tannhäuser (Singers' Hall with a view of the castle in the background) and Lohengrin (castle courtyard, open corridor, path to the chapel); this castle will be in every way more beautiful and habitable than Hohenschwangau further down, which is desecrated every year by the prose of my mother; they will take revenge, the desecrated gods, and come to live with Us on the lofty heights, breathing the air of heaven«.

Design for the window arcades on the first floor of the Knights' House by the architect Julius Hofmann, 1884, with abstract plants and animals

*Plan of 1820 with views and ground plans of the ruins Hinter- and Vorderhohenschwangau over which Neuschwanstein Castle was built;*

After the disappointments and setbacks early on in his reign, the king increasingly withdrew from public life to the seclusion of the mountains he loved so much. It was here, in the area he had known since he was a child, that he decided to build a new residence. His father Maximilian II had acquired Schwanstein, the seat of the knights of Schwangau, in 1832 when he was still crown prince, with the idea of »restoring [the ruin] to its original medi-

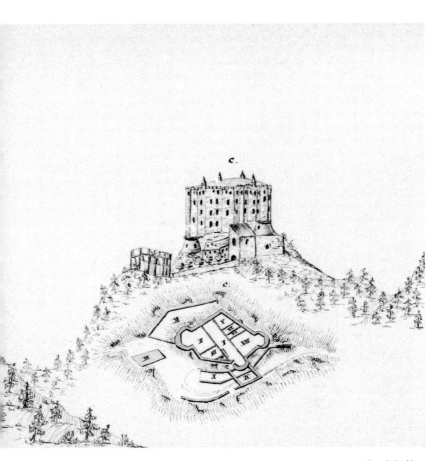

eval form«. The result was the present Hohenschwangau Castle, built from plans by the set-designer Domenico Quaglio. Maximilian II ordered the construction of paths and lookout points in the area around Hohenschwangau to enable him to enjoy the scenery, and also had the iron bridge, the »Marienbrücke«, built above the Pöllat Gorge for his consort Marie. In 1855 he made plans to build a viewing pavilion on a narrow ridge high above this gorge, which commanded a magnificent view of the whole area and was originally the location of the medieval castle Vorderhohenschwangau. This never progressed beyond the planning stage. In 1867 Ludwig II decided to »rebuild« Vorderhohenschwangau as his castle. In the building documents of 1868 the project was still called »Restoration of the old ruined castle«, although what was left of the medieval building was eventually removed to make way for the new building.

*Oriel in the bedroom, stained-glass windows with the Wittelsbach, Bavarian and Schwangau coats of arms, upholstery embroidered with crowns, lions, swans and lilies*

## SWAN KNIGHT

In Neuschwanstein the late romantic concept of restoration, which makes a further appearance in 1883 in Ludwig's plans for Falkenstein Castle, is combined with the idea of a new castle of the swan knight Lohengrin. The knight's heraldic animal, the swan, had already featured as a leitmotif in the castle built by Ludwig's father, a building which had had a substantial influence on the development of Ludwig's artistic tastes. The swan was also the historic heraldic animal of the knights of Schwangau. Maximilian saw himself as their successor and adopted their coat of arms. His son followed suit, and the swan thus also features as a heraldic animal in Neuschwanstein; it is sometimes used in combination with the medieval coat of arms of the Pfalzgraf bei Rhein, a title still held by Ludwig, and the lozengy of the royal coat-of-arms of Bavaria. Ludwig II had been familiar with the Lohengrin legend since he was a child from the murals of his father's castle. He was introduced to Wagner's »Lohengrin« on 2 February 1861 in the Munich Court Opera House and was captivated. Thus, in the course of time, Ludwig II came to see himself in typically romantic fashion as both a real knight of Schwangau and the fictitious swan knight Lohengrin, while always remaining fully conscious of himself as the ruling king of Bavaria.

The scene painter Christian Jank, who produced the first drawings for Neuschwanstein, clearly based the castle courtyard on the stage set of the 2nd act of the opera »Lohengrin«, »Courtyard of Antwerp Castle« as designed by Angelo II Quaglio for the Munich Lohengrin production of 1867. A reference to Act 3 in the form of a bedroom resembling the bridal chamber for Elsa and Lohengrin was to be incorporated in the Bower. However, as shown by the letter to Wagner quoted above, the king visualized Neuschwanstein not only as Lohengrin's castle, but also as Tannhäuser's. Ludwig was involved in the preparation of a new production of »Tannhäuser« and, at Wagner's suggestion, went on 31 May 1867

Richard Wagner. Photograph by Pierre Petit & Trinquart, Paris 1860

Right side: King Ludwig II in civilian attire. Photograph by Joseph Albert, March 1867

to visit the scene of the historic Singers' Contest, the Wartburg. A prime example of the tendency in Germany to romanticize all things medieval, this castle had been »reconstructed« in the same year. For Ludwig it represented an authentic combination of the Middle Ages and the artistic celebration of minnesong and knighthood which prevailed in this era. It was exactly this combination he was aiming for, and the romantically »reconstructed« Wartburg gave him ideas as to how he might achieve it. From the beginning the Neuschwanstein project included a Singers' Hall modelled on the Banqueting Hall of the Wartburg, although the latter was not com-

Pages above:
Model of the set
for Act 2 of the
opera Lohengrin
designed for the
new Munich pro-
duction of 1867
and built by An-
gelo II Quaglio in
1866; some of
the motifs were
incorporated in
Neuschwanstein.

pleted until 1876. In 1858 King Friedrich Wilhelm IV of Prussia expressly ordered the plans for this Wartburg hall to be used for the set of Act 2 in the first Berlin production of »Tannhäuser«. Ludwig had a new Singers' Hall constructed for Neuschwanstein which was designed by Jank and was a combination of the Festival Hall and the Singers' Bower of the medieval Singers' Hall in the Wartburg. The Neuschwanstein Singers' Hall also became the model for subsequent »Tannhäuser« sets. The building which combined all the scenes from »Lohengrin« and »Tannhäuser« would not of course have been complete without the »Grotto in the Hörselberg«. From 1880 the room next to Ludwig II's study was transformed into a small artificial grotto with a waterfall by a landscape sculptor, or scenic sculptor in modern theatre terminology. As a result of his lifelong fascination with Wagner's work, Ludwig II was always a very generous patron of the 19th century's leading music dramatist. The premières of »Tristan und Isolde«, »Die Meistersinger von Nürnberg«, »Rheingold« and »Walküre« also had epochmaking sets due to the very high standards set by Ludwig, and for a short period from 1865 to 1870 Munich as a result became the music capital of Europe. Without Ludwig II, neither Wagner's late works nor the Bayreuth festival would ever have come into being. Ludwig II was personally involved in the composition of Wagner's last work for the stage, »Parsifal«: in the final years of his life he identified himself with this figure, and he was also regarded in this light by Wagner, a fact of which Ludwig was aware. This explains the mural programme of the Singers' Hall and its function as a monument.

## ROMANESQUE AND ROMANTIC

The government architect selected to convert Christian Jank's pictorial representations into plans was Eduard

Riedel, who had already redesigned Berg Palace for Ludwig's father in 1849–51. In accordance with the king's wishes, Jank turned the »robber knight's castle« with late gothic elements that he had originally designed into a monumental »Romanesque« castle with a five-storey Palas in the general style of the Wartburg Palas. Neuschwanstein, which everyone now oddly enough thinks of as a typical »medieval castle«, is thus not a copy of any existing building, but a characteristic example of historicism, in which architectural motifs from the Wartburg are combined with those of castles from medieval book illustrations. It is significant that Jank's project was criticized for not being faithful to history. The painter Michael Welter, who was recommended to the king by the castellan of Wartburg for his historical accuracy, undertook to provide the »necessary details« for Neuschwanstein based on Romanesque examples and declared that Jank's final designs would »incite the most virulent and bitter criticism«. Court secretary Düfflipp turned down Welter's proposals in a letter of 21 November 1871, for the following most revealing reasons: »It is the will of His Majesty the King that the new castle be built in the Romanesque style. We are now living in the year 1871, centuries after the period of the Romanesque style, and there can be no doubt that the achievements that have since been attained in the areas of art and science will also benefit us in the construction of this building. – By this I do not in the least mean that we should alter the style itself in a way that would impair its character, but neither do I mean that we should recreate the old days in every respect and not benefit from experience which would have been made use of them, had it been available«. Historicism frequently involved not just copying the historical styles, but »perfecting« them using all the latest craft skills and technical means. For this reason the typical combination of modern (building) technology and historic architectural and furnishing styles was

Ideal design for Neuschwanstein Castle by Christian Jank in 1868, which incorporated Richard Wagner's instructions for the set of Act 2 of the opera Lohengrin; east view of the Upper Courtyard, with the keep and chapel in the centre

by no means considered a contradiction. This was also Ludwig II's philosophy, so that the »Romanesque« castle of Neuschwanstein has a very modern kitchen, hot air heating, and numerous large, tightly-fitting windows with frames made of industrial steel.

The exterior of the castle became increasingly austere when Georg Dollmann succeeded Riedel in 1874 and many of the picturesque details in Jank's designs were dropped. In the sections completed in simplified form after 1886 this tendency increased.

Julius Hofmann, who completed the complex on the basis of Riedel's plans from 1886 to 1892, designed the entire »Romanesque« interior of Neuschwanstein complete with furnishing in accordance with the king's ideas. Only the bedroom, designed by Peter Herwegen, and the adjacent chapel are in late-gothic style with furniture that is comparatively historic by comparison with the Biedermeier neo-gothic interiors of Hohenschwangau.

*Mural »Lohengrin's arrival« (in Brabant) by August von Heckel, 1880/81, in the salon*

## MURALS

The king checked every detail of the interior from the drafts and frequently ordered corrections to be made before work could begin. He was particularly involved with the planning of the murals. His father had similarly decorated Hohenschwangau with murals of local legends, some of them from sketches by Moritz von Schwind. Ludwig II consulted the literary historian Dr. Hyazinth Holland, a specialist in medieval iconography, who provided him with a wide variety of possible themes, but the motifs he chose for the castle were almost exclusively related to Wagner's music dramas. However, in 1879 he had already decreed that »the pictures in the new castle should be based on the original legends and not on Wagner's interpretation of them«. It was thus Ludwig's conscious wish to go back to the historic sources of Wagner's

work. For this he wanted »only painters who make an exact study of the medieval poetry«, in other words painters of historical scenes, who kept strictly to the concept derived by the king from his literary studies and based on the principle of poetic glorification of a real or imagined historical truth. This was however no different from what was generally expected of the specialized painters of historical scenes throughout the 19th century.

## THRONE HALL

Even later on in the proceedings, the whole Neuschwanstein programme frequently had to be altered as the king's concept of it changed. Years before the premiere in Bayreuth, he was already studying the stage set for Wagner's »Parsifal« and in 1876 he asked Eduard Ille to design him a Grail Hall in Byzantine style, based on Hagia Sophia in Constantinople. From this he developed the idea of a Throne Hall in Neuschwanstein. In the final design for this room, by Julius Hofmann, which was only completed in 1881 and also incorporated medieval descriptions of the legendary Grail Hall, the »Wartburg« designed for the young king was transformed into Parzival's »Castle of the Holy Grail«. The six canonized kings featured in the apse, whose deeds are depicted in the hall's murals, represented Ludwig II's idea of pure kingship »by the Grace of God«. The figures beneath the cupola representing the pre-Christian cultures and realms of India, Rome, Greece, Persia and Egypt and »The moral code of the Old Testament« on the opposite wall symbolize the secular and sacred basis of the Christian kingdom. On the floor is a mosaic of concentrically ordered animals and plants which shows that Ludwig II, who designed the complex programme of the hall himself, was also well versed in Buddhist and Oriental philosophy. In the cupola directly above the life cycle on the floor is the sun, indicating that kingship is part of a cos-

*Mosaic on the floor of the Throne Hall with plants and animals, coloured pen-and-ink drawing by Julius Hofmann, 1883; the mosaic produced by Anton Detoma in 1885/87 is almost identical.*

*Following pages: South view of the Throne Hall with chandelier in the form of a crown by Eduard Wollenweber, columns with coloured stucco-work, ornamental painting and murals on a gold background, 1885/86*

# Julius Hofmann (1840–1896)

The architect Julius Hofmann trained in Vienna. In 1864 he worked for Maximilian, Archduke of Austria and Emperor of Mexico. From 1867 on he was employed in the service of Ludwig II, first as a colleague of Georg Dollmann, and from 1884 as court architect.

Hofmann was in charge of building Neuschwanstein, and also drew up plans for the interior of every room in the castle, which other artists and their workshops were commissioned to produce. The extremely versatile Hofmann designed not only the furniture, textiles, murals and sculptures, but everything down to the washstand set in

the king's bedroom and the glass paintings in the windows. As a typical representative of historicism he based his work on historic styles, with a preference for the Romanesque and gothic eras, while also including elements of non-European architecture taken from Chinese pavilions and Arabic mosques.

Hofmann's designs also confirm him in many respects as a forerunner and pioneer of art nouveau.

*Design for the throne canopy (not constructed) in the Throne Hall; on the upholstered back of the throne is the monogram of Ludwig II. Coloured pen-and-ink drawing by Julius Hofmann, 1884* mological whole. This room, which was not merely a throne hall but rather a temple to kingship, sums up Ludwig II's complex view of the world. In addition to this, however, this unique cult centre and monument to kingship also incorporates the dynasty of the ruling king of Bavaria: Ludwig II expressly requested the inclusion of clear references to the All Saints Church in the Munich Residence, built in the Byzantine style by his grandfather Ludwig I from 1826. The composition of the apse painting was taken from another of Ludwig I's churches, St Bonifaz in Munich, in which he is buried.

The original programme was changed and the Singers' Hall was now designed to prepare the way for the Throne Hall; in 1883–84 it was decorated with murals presenting the Parzival saga according to Wolfram von Eschenbach. In the Singers' Bower Parzival appears as the King of the Holy Grail, and the opposite wall shows his son Lohengrin departing from the Castle of the Holy Grail. The picture programme thus comes full circle and links up with the swan knight theme which was the starting point of Neuschwanstein.

## HISTORICISM AND THE MODERN AGE

The Throne Hall of Neuschwanstein, which was to have been completed in the year of Ludwig II's death and never had its throne, is the only one of the king's Byzantine projects that was ever completed. Two large Byzantine palaces were designed for him, first in 1869 by Georg Dollmann and again towards the end of his life in 1885 by Julius Hofmann, which were intended to manifest his kingship by God's grace, as was also the very different palace of Herrenchiemsee. Both were to have been built in the Graswangtal near Lin-

*Three-legged candelabra in the Throne Hall with Romanesque and Art Nouveau elements, designed by Julius Hofmann in 1884 and made by Eduard Wollenweber in gilt brass with Bohemian glass stones*

*Ideal design for a Grail Hall, produced in 1876 by Eduard Ille for Ludwig II and based on medieval descriptions, with Byzantine architectural motifs. The king primarily wanted a reproduction of the Grail Hall described by Albrecht von Scharfenberg in »Titurel«.*

derhof Palace. Since Falkenstein Castle near Pfronten also never progressed beyond the planning stage, Neuschwanstein remained in many respects a unique monument to one of the greatest builders from the House of Wittelsbach, whose works are also different because of their relationship to the theatre. At the same time, as a main work of historicism Neuschwanstein also underlines the unmistakable achievements of 19th-century art, with, for example, the surprisingly early manifestations of art nouveau in Jank's architectural features or in details of Hofmann's interior such as the »Romanesque« chandeliers of the Throne Hall. In addition the very latest technology was used, such as the steel construction for the Throne Hall and the multicoloured electric lighting in the grotto, often only being incorporated for the purpose of illusion. For the king however, his palaces and castles – which by contrast with most royal buildings were not intended for the public – were more than an illusion, more than an imaginary world into which he withdrew out of protest against a bourgeois world that did not understand him. They were his life and a setting in which history was to be resurrected – just as it was on the stage of his court theatre. Ludwig II, who by no means ruined the state financially with his projects, as is often maintained, but paid for everything out of his own pocket, applied himself to these undertakings with great skill and an energy which he often lacked in political matters. When foreign creditor banks forced him to stop building by threatening to seize his property, life lost its purpose for the king, who made his last journey from Neuschwanstein to Berg on 12 June 1886 after being declared insane. Thus the king, who could not cope with the role of a monarch in a constitutional monarchy, and was called the »only true king of this century« by Paul Verlaine in a sonnet of 1886, finally perished because, with a lack of compromise shown by none of his contemporaries, he created an alternative world in which he could live as the absolutist or medieval king of Bavaria.

# Planning history

In 1867 Ludwig II collected numerous ideas for the buildings he was planning. While he was making a study of Versailles, he also asked to be shown round Pierrefond Castle, which the famous architect Viollet-le-Duc had only recently »reconstructed« in medieval style. Viollet's encyclopaedic publications on historic styles were a further source of ideas for Ludwig II's Neuschwanstein. The Festival Hall and Singers' Hall of the Wartburg were a fixed part of the programme from start to finish, while other rooms were dropped from the plans or substantially altered.

The architect Eduard Riedel was instructed by Ludwig II to make drawings of the Wartburg, while Christian Jank produced drawings of the Romanesque ornamentation. The architect and artist worked closely together. Riedel dealt with the practical architectural aspects of Ludwig's historically-oriented specifications, such as the structural engineering, development and functions. Jank then turned the plans into picturesque views, since the king, who was a very visual person, always wanted to know exactly what his buildings were going to look like. The first drafts of the new castle are predominantly influenced by the Wartburg, but have been adapted to the existing foundations of the two medieval ruins: here the two main buildings, the Palas and the keep (a separate construction), stand one behind the other. The palace chapel was to be located on the ground floor of the keep. The plans were then soon expanded as the king elaborated on his original ideas and new building sections were added: the Knights' House on the north side, the Bower on the south side and the Gateway Building on the east side, as well as an increasing number of towers. The

*Preliminary design for Neuschwanstein from 1868 by Christian Jank; based on the two ruined castles on the site, it is much smaller than the final building.*

external resemblance to the Wartburg was thus reduced to specific details such as the Romanesque windows. The 1868 plans were no longer based on the medieval foundations of Vorderhohenschwangau, so that the original idea of reconstructing it was in fact dropped at an early stage of the proceedings.

The Palas was initially to have four floors, with »guest rooms« on the first floor, the »Large Banqueting Hall« based on the Singers' Hall in the Wartburg on the second floor, and the »Apartment« of the king on the third floor. The names of the rooms show that at this stage Ludwig II was still envisaging social activities at his castle. By 1868 the plans for the Palas had already been expanded: the room now called the »Festival Hall« was located on a fourth floor and had slanting ceilings like the Festival Hall of the Wartburg, and a »Dining Room« was added on the west side of the building, with an »Audience Room« and two anterooms beneath it on the third floor. As the years passed, the king became increasingly isolated; from 1878 the »Dining Room«, »Audience Room«

*The Wartburg from the east, on the left the Palas with the Festival Hall and Singers' Hall, in the centre the keep, on the right the Vorburg (front castle)*

*Left side: Design for the viewing terrace west of the Palas, also drawn in section, by Julius Hofmann, 1884/85*

Design drawing
of one of the
iron supports of
the Throne Hall,
section and out-
lines, produced
by the Royal
Architectural
Office in 1882

Following pages:
Neuschwanstein
under construc-
tion with the
Square Tower
and the founda-
tions covered
with scaffolding;
photograph
taken early in
1886

and anterooms were replaced with the two-storey Throne Hall, from which all outsiders were excluded, and from 1882 a »Moorish Hall« was planned on the second floor in place of the guest rooms. This hall was never built, neither was the bathing hall with a terrace in front of it on the floor below. The large keep with the castle chapel planned for the east side of the Upper Courtyard opposite the Palas was also never built.

## BUILDING HISTORY

Work on the future building site began in the summer of 1868 with up to 8 metres of stone outcrop removed to make way for the foundations. In June 1869 the new access road was completed. The foundation stone was laid on 5 September 1869 with the building plan, portraits of Ludwig II and coins from his reign incorporated in it in accordance with the tradition established by Ludwig I. The latest building techniques and materials were used in the construction of the castle. The foundations were cemented and the walls built of brick with light-coloured limestone used merely as cladding. The Gateway Building was completed first, which had its topping out ceremony on 11 June 1872 and was ready for occupation at the end of 1873; for years Ludwig II used the upper floor as provisional accommodation when he visited the site. Building of the Palas commenced in September 1872; for structural reasons the latest technology was required in order to incorporate the large Throne Hall subsequently requested by the king, which was built as an encased steel construction. The topping out ceremony was on 29 January, 1880. The decoration and technical fittings of the interior were only completed in mid 1884, though without all the final details. Ludwig II only ever saw his new castle as a building site; the Bower and the Square Tower, simplified versions of the original-ly planned buildings, were not completed until 1892.

# Exterior

The castle complex occupies a narrow, 1008-metre ridge with steep sides and a backdrop of rugged mountain scenery. It consists of the Gateway Building at the eastern end, the Bower to the south, the Knights' House with the Square Tower to the north and the Palas with two towers at the western end. With the exception of the Gateway Building, the exterior is clad with white limestone, making it visible for miles around.

*South view of Neuschwanstein Castle from the Marien-Brücke; from left to right: Palas, Bower, Square Tower and Gateway Building*

## NORTHERN FAÇADE (FROM THE FINAL BEND OF THE ACCESS ROAD)

From left to right: north corner tower of the Gateway Building, Lower Connecting Building, Square Tower, Upper Connecting Building, Knight's House with staircase tower, north façade of the eastern Palas section with Conservatory, rectangular staircase tower with statue of the Madonna, study balcony, octagonal staircase tower (65 m) with statue of St George and north façade of the Throne Hall tract. All the exterior statues are by Philipp Perron.

## WESTERN FAÇADE (FROM THE PATH TO THE MARIENBRÜCKE)

The western façade ends in a gable with two square corner turrets, which is crowned with a copper-embossed statue of a knight. On the northwestern corner is a stone statue of St Cecilia. Two-storey balcony in front of the Throne Hall with arcades on masked consoles. The door on the ground floor was originally intended to lead onto a terrace, but this was never constructed.

## SOUTHERN FAÇADE (FROM THE MARIENBRÜCKE)

*Upper Courtyard with Bower, Knights' House and Palas; the foundations of the castle chapel that was never built are visible on the ground.*

Impressive view of the castle complex across the precipitous Pöllat Gorge, with the flat countryside surrounding the town of Füssen beyond. From left to right: Palas with round staircase tower and the oriel and balcony of the bedroom, Bower with square staircase tower and octagonal projection, square tower of the Knight's House, southern corner tower of the Gateway Building. A crevasse with bridged by the foundations of the castle can be seen below the Bower.

## EASTERN FAÇADE (VISITORS' ENTRANCE; SEE COVER PICTURE)

Two-storey, crenellated Gateway Building with round corner towers and a three-storey middle section with a crow-stepped gable. The towers and the projecting gate section are clad with white limestone, the middle section with decorative bricks and Molasse sandstone. Over the gateway is the Bavarian royal coat of arms, above which is a gallery with two balcony-like corner projections.

## LOWER COURTYARD

On the east side is the Gateway Building, on the north side the Connecting Building with an outside staircase to the Gateway Building and Square Tower, on the west side a wall with pillars and a fountain and an outside staircase leading to the Upper Courtyard, on the south side a low wall facing the Pöllat Gorge.

Entrance hall of the Gateway Building with groined vault; on the portal of the guards' room the relief of a dog

with the circumscription »Fidelity is vigilant day and night«. Courtyard façade clad with white limestone and yellowish Rhaetic sandstone. On the second floor is a balcony with colonnades. The rooms on this floor, which are not accessible, served as provisional accommodation for the king while the Palas apartments were under construction; in the rooms on the first floor the government commission which was to declare Ludwig II unfit to govern was for a short time held captive.

The 45-metre Square Tower ends with a projecting gallery and a cylindrical, crenellated top section.

The projecting section of the wall was originally intended as the foundation of the choir in the palace chapel that was to have been located on the ground floor of the keep; the keep, however, was never built.

## UPPER COURTYARD

*Embossed copper lion on the east gable of the Palas, with a symmetrical mane in medieval style*

On the west side is the gable façade of the Palas, on the south side the Bower, on the east side the low parapet of the wall, on the north side the Connecting Building with the Knights' House. The foundation walls of the keep are marked out on the ground.

An outside staircase leads up to the main portal of the Palas on the first floor. Façade with two-storey oriels; above the balcony of the Singers' Hall are two frescoes, »St George« and »Patrona Bavariae«, by Wilhelm Hauschild; gable crowned by a copper-embossed lion.

The Bower was only completed in its present form in 1892. According to the 1885 plans, the façade

*Console busts in late medieval style under the balcony oriel of the Palas*

was to have ornamental sculpture and statues of female saints. Central projection with portal and balcony. On the west side an outside staircase leading to the first floor.

In the middle of the two-storey Connecting Building between the Palas and the Square Tower is the three-storey Knights' House with a gable. The building has the same windows, modelled on the Wartburg, as the rest of the castle; it was completed without the naturalistic ornamentation originally planned for the first floor.

# Rooms

*Pages above:
Throne Hall with
apse; mural of
Christ as ruler
of the world with
Mary and John
the Baptist, be-
neath them
between palm
trees six canon-
ized kings*

On the first floor of the so-called Palas (the residential part of a medieval castle) are the servants' quarters, with authentic furnishings. The rooms in the Palas are accessed via the two staircase towers in the northwest and southeast. The rooms on the second floor were never finished and are today used for administrative purposes.

The apartments and state rooms of the king are on the third and fourth floors and the interiors were more or less complete by 1886. All the rooms are dominated by paintings, which cover the walls and ceilings and include elements taken from Persian and medieval book illustration, and decorative carving. Every detail of the interior was designed by Julius Hofmann (see box), and produced by other artists and workshops. The imposing chandeliers and candelabras of gilt brass in the Throne Room, the Singers' Hall and the king's apartments are from Eduard Wollenweber's workshop, and the elaborate door fittings are by Karl Moradelli. Max Steinmetz produced the magnificently embroidered textiles.

## 1 LOWER HALL

The Palas consists of two sections, which meet at an obtuse angle due to the limitations of the ridge-top site. The hall, connecting the two parts, thus narrows at one end. Marble portals open into the Throne Room on the west side and the royal apartments on the opposite side. On the walls are illustrations of the Sigurd saga from the Old Norse saga »Edda«, a collection of sagas, songs and sayings. Sigurd corresponds to the Siegfried of the Middle High German Nibelungenlied.

Murals of the Sigurd legend by Wilhelm Hauschild, Karl Schultheiß, Josef Munsch and Ferdinand Piloty (1882/83). The brothers Fafnir and Regin are in possession of a hoard of golden treasure, the Nibelungen treasure, on which, however, the gods have laid a curse. Fafnir seizes the treasure for himself and turns himself into a dragon to guard it. Regin forges the beautiful sword Gram and gives it to the young king Sigurd, who uses it to kill Fafnir but then also Regin, and thus acquires the fateful treasure. (»Gripyn prophesies Sigurd's fate« ■ »Regin forges the sword Gram for Sigurd« ■ »Sigurd kills Fafnir«). Sigurd finds the sleeping Valkyrie Brynhild confined within a ring of fire and pledges to be true to her. Continuing on his journey, he reaches the kingdom of Franconia on the Rhine. The king's daughter Gudrun gives him a magic potion which makes him forget Brynhild and marry her instead. (»Sigurd rides through the raging fire to Brynhild« ■ »Gudrun gives Sigurd the po-

*Door fittings decorated with leaves and tendrils and handles in the form of swans' heads by Karl Moradelli*

48

tion«). Now Gudrun's brother Gunnar wants to win Brynhild. He can only do this with Sigurd's help, and Brynhild demands atonement for the humiliation she has suffered at Sigurd's hands. The youngest of Gudrun's brothers, Guttorm, is forced to kill Sigurd. Brynhild kills herself with the sword and is burned with Sigurd on the same pyre. (»Sigurd's death« ■ »Gudrun awaits Sigurd's return« ■ »Brynhild scorns Gunnar« ■ »Gudrun's lament over Sigurd's body« ■ »Sigurd and Brynhild are burned together on the same pyre«).

Painted, wrought-iron chandelier with swan motif by Karl Moradelli.

*Mural in the Lower Hall illustrating the Sigurd-legend: »Gudrun's lament over Sigurd's body«, 1882/83*

## 2 THRONE HALL

This sumptuous, church-like hall with its massive, four-metre high chandelier occupies the third and fourth floors and the entire west section of the Palas.

The Throne Hall was inspired by Byzantine churches and in particular the All Saints Court Church in Munich. In the northern apse there was to be a throne in place of the altar, but this was never constructed after the death of the king. This combination of church and throne room illustrates Ludwig's interpretation of kingship: he saw himself not just as a king by God's grace, but also as a mediator between God and the whole world. This idea is also expressed in the cupola, which is decorated with stars, and the floor mosaic beneath it, which shows the earth with its plants and animals. Beneath the cupola are representatives of pre-Christian kingdoms. The pictures in the apse area show Christ, the Twelve Apostles and six holy kings, while the deeds of the kings and other saints are illustrated on the walls. The Throne Hall was not intended for state occasions. It is an expression of Ludwig's expectations of kingship.

Murals by Wilhelm Hauschild, Waldemar Kolmsperger and other artists. In the apse: »Christ in his glory, with John and Mary,

49

Mural in the Throne Hall: »St George killing the dragon« by Waldemar Kolmsperger, 1884, with the silhouette of Falkenstein Castle, which Ludwig II also planned to build, in the background

Following pages: View of the dining room with the original furnishings (historical photograph); today the table has been moved to the side to create a passage through the room.

symbols of the Evangelists and angels«; beneath these figures are six canonized kings: »Kasimir of Poland« ■ »Stephen I of Hungary« ■ »Emperor Heinrich II« ■ »Louis IX of France« ■ »Ferdinand III of Spain« ■ »Edward the Confessor of England«; next to the throne steps: »The Twelve Apostles«. In the arcades: »King Edward of England as a righteous knight« ■ »King Ferdinand of Spain fighting the Moors« ■ »St George« (in the background the silhouette of Falkenstein Castle near Pfronten, which Ludwig II planned to build within sight of Neuschwanstein) ■ »Landgravine Elisabeth von Thüringen performing charitable works« ■ »Queen Clothilde of France converts her husband to Christianity«. On the gallery: »Conversion of the Hungarians by King Stephen of Hungary« ■ »Emperor Heinrich II as a founder of churches« ■ »St Michael« ■ »King Louis IX of France as a benefactor«. Under the vault: »Ancient law« ■ »The moral law of the Old Testament«.

### ▣ ANTEROOM

The apartments of Ludwig II are entered through the oak-panelled anteroom on the third floor. An electric bell system was installed in 1885 so that the servant on duty here could be summoned from any other room.

### ▣ DINING ROOM

Wolfram von Eschenbach and other minnesingers feature in the dining room murals, which are framed with oak panelling decorated with bas-relief carvings. On the dining table is a centrepiece in marble and gilt bronze, which shows Siegfried fighting the dragon. As in all the king's rooms, the textiles are very elaborate; here they are made of red silk with gold embroidery and trimmings.

Murals by Ferdinand Piloty and Josef Aigner: »Landgrave Hermann presents gifts to minstrels« ■ »Gottfried von Straßburg«

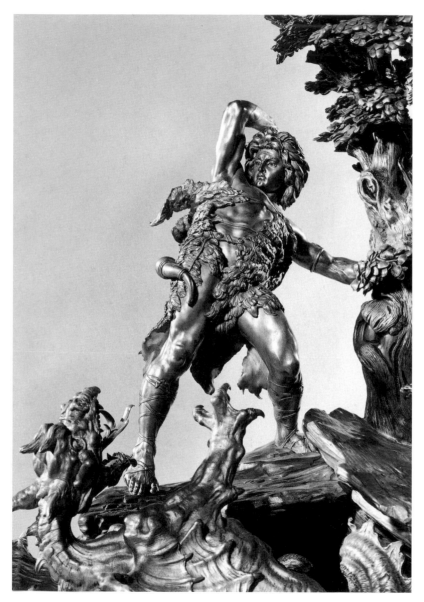

■ »Heinrich von Veldeke's poem Äneïde is returned to him by the Landgrave after its rediscovery« ■ »The sorcerer Klingsor, disguised as an oriental merchant, sets the court riddles to solve« ■ »Wolfram von Eschenbach« ■ »Singers' Contest at the Wartburg« ■ »The sorcerer Klingsor brings Heinrich von Ofterdingen to the Wartburg« ■ »Reinmar von Zweter« ■ »The Landgrave commissions Wolfram von Eschenbach to translate the poem ›Willehalm‹ « ■ »Performance by minstrels at the Landgrave's court«. In the quatrefoils above the window arches: »Prudence and Temperance« ■ »Justice and Valour«.

Centrepiece by Eduard Wollenweber from a model by Ludwig Bierling, 1885/86.

## ▄5▄ BEDROOM

As in all the residences of Ludwig II, the king's bedroom is particularly sumptuous. The leitmotif is the legend of Tristan and Isolde, and the two main characters feature not only in the murals, but also in the carvings on the door and the ceramic figures on the tiled stove. The state bed in the neo-gothic style and the seat coverings are in blue silk, with embroidered and appliquéd lions, swans, crowns, lilies and the Bavarian coat of arms. One of the most unusual features is the washstand, with a fountain in the form of a silver-plated swan. Small swans also decorate the washstand set – water jug, sponge and soap containers – which was designed by Eduard Wollenweber.

Murals of the Tristan legend by August Spieß (1881): Tristan travels to Ireland to win the hand of the beautiful Isolde for King Marke of Cornwall. On their way back Tristan drinks a goblet of wine with Isolde which, unknown to them, is a love potion (»Tristan gives Isolde the love potion«). The lovers meet secretly in the garden of the castle in Cornwall, although Isolde is now married to King Marke. Here Marke takes them by surprise and Tristan is seriously injured by Marke's liegeman Melot in a duel

*Centrepiece in gilt bronze: »Siegfried fighting the dragon«, designed by Ludwig Bierling for the dining room table and made by Eduard Wollenweber, 1885/86*

*Following pages: Bedroom with murals of Tristan und Isolde, oak furniture and carvings by Anton Pössenbacher, washstand with silver-plated swan fountain designed by Julius Hofmann*

*Madonna, 1883, modelled on a figure in Hagia Sophia, bed headboard, Andreas Müller*

*Right side: Armchair with baldachin and reading table in a style resembling that of a medieval priedieu; view from the window of the Pollät Gorge with the Marienbrücke*

(»Tristan bids farewell to Isolde« ■ »Tristan and Isolde in the garden of the Cornwall castle«). Kurwenal brings the dying Tristan to Kareol, to the castle of his fathers. King Marke learns that a magic potion was the cause of his wife's unfaithfulness and travels to Kareol to forgive the lovers. But it is too late: Tristan dies of his injuries and Isolde of grief (»Tristan waiting for Isolde« ■ »Isolde's arrival with Kurwenal« ■ »Tristan and Isolde united in death«). ■ »Lady reading Tristan« ■ »Faithfulness« ■ »Love«.

All the oak furniture in the room is by Anton Pössenbacher, 1883.

The oratory adjacent to the bedroom is also in the neo-gothic style. The murals, glass windows and the middle picture on the altar feature Louis IX of France, the patron saint of the king. There was a further connection between Ludwig II and the ruling Bourbon family: King Louis XVI – a direct descendant of Louis IX – was the godfather of his grandfather King Ludwig I.

*Oratory, with walls, altar and glass windows decorated with pictures of St Louis, the patron saint of Ludwig II*

Painting on the winged altar and murals by Wilhelm Hauschild: »St Louis« ▪ »The death of Tristan, the son of St Louis« ▪ »St Louis receives the Banner of the Cross«.
Glass painting from the Mayer'sche Hofkunstanstalt (1882): »St Louis receiving extreme unction«.
Ivory crucifix by Anton Dießl, 1883.

**7** DRESSING ROOM

The dressing room is decorated in the style of a garden hall with an illusionistic ceiling painting of a garden bower with a trellis of vines open to the sky. The murals between the panelling show scenes from the life and poems of Walther von der Vogelweide (ca. 1170–1230) and Hans Sachs (1494–1576). Above the arch leading to the oriel recess are half-length portraits of both poets. The seat covers and the curtains are made of violet silk magnificently embroidered in gold with an elaborate design of leaves, tendrils and pairs of peacocks. In the oriel recess is the king's jewelry box.

Murals by Eduard Ille (pupil of Moritz von Schwind): »The birds teach Walther von der Vogelweide how to sing« ▪ »Walther sings his song in praise of German morals at the court of Duke Guelph« ▪ »Walther wins the support of the German princes for the crusade« ▪ »Walther on his journeys« ▪ »I sat on a rock...«

■ »Walther participating in a crusade« ■ »Under the linden-tree...« ■ »Hans Sachs performing a song to an audience that includes Pirkheimer, Peter Vischer and Dürer« ■ »Sachs presenting a young singer with the master's chain« ■ »Sachs with his friends« ■ »Sachs in his study«.

## 8 SALON

The L-shaped salon has an alcove furnished with chairs and separated from the rest of the room by columns. The large oak cupboard is modelled on an item of furniture from the Wartburg and is decorated with scenes from medieval poems. The murals in this room show scenes

*Right side: Dressing room with illusionistic ceiling painting and murals of scenes from the lives and poems of Walther von der Vogelweide and Hans Sachs*

*Ludwig II's jewel casket with a painting of a medieval theme, »Droit du seigneur«, in the oriel recess of the dressing room, 1884/86*

*Following pages: Salon with alcove, murals of the Lohengrin legend and blue silk textiles embroidered with swans and lilies*

62

from the Lohengrin saga, which Ludwig II identified with in particular on account of the Grail Knight theme and the swan motif. The swan was also Ludwig's heraldic animal as a Knight of Schwangau. As in the bedroom, the curtains and coverings are made of blue silk and embroidered with swans and lilies. There is also a container for plants or flowers in the form of a large majolica swan by Villeroy & Boch.

*Artificial grotto by August Dirigl with coloured lighting, a reproduction of the Hörselberg (or Venus Mountain) from the Tannhäuser legend*

Murals of the Lohengrin saga by Wilhelm Hauschild and August von Heckel: The Knight Lohengrin is selected through the miracle of the Grail to protect the king's daughter Elsa (»Miracle of the Grail« ■ »Lohengrin's arrival« ■ »Elsa tells Lohengrin her troubles«). In a duel he defeats Count Telramund, who has accused Elsa of fratricide and wants to become king himself (»Elsa asks Lohengrin for his support« ■ »Lohengrin lands at Antwerp« ■ »The mass before the duel« ■ »Arrival of the contestants« ■ »Duel with Telramund«). Elsa and Lohengrin marry, although she knows nothing about his origins and must never ask. After they are married, Elsa nevertheless asks Lohengrin the fateful question. The swan which brought Lohengrin then reappears and changes into Elsa's missing brother. Lohengrin, however, must return to the Castle of the Holy Grail (»Lohengrin weds Elsa« ■ »Elsa goes to the cathedral« ■ »Elsa's question« ■ »Transformation of the swan«).
Pictures on the cupboard doors by Ferdinand Piloty: »Gottfried von Straßburg with lady and monk« ■ »Wolfram von Eschenbach presents his Parzival poem to the Landgrave of Thüringen« ■ »The legendary blind poet of the Nibelungenlied with Bishop Pilgrim and scribe«.

## ▣ GROTTO AND CONSERVATORY

Between the salon and the study is a room that would not normally be found in a royal apartment: a small grotto. The set-designer August Dirigl created the artificial dripstone cave, which originally had coloured lighting and a water-

*Writing desk, chairs, stool and writing set with Lohengrin sculpture in the study by Philipp Perron and Ferdinand Harrach, 1883 (historical photograph)*

*Right side: Study with murals of the Tannhäuser legend; like all the rooms of the royal apartments, it has an elaborately carved and painted ceiling.*

fall. It was based on the idea of the Hörselberg in the Tannhäuser saga. The adjacent glassed-in balcony housed the king's conservatory; the small fountain was intended for a Moorish Hall, which was not however completed.

## ▣ STUDY

The murals show the Tannhäuser saga. As in the opera of the same name, this is linked with the Singers' Contest on the Wartburg. The king worked at the large table in the centre of the room, on which his writing set still stands. The cupboard was used to store the castle plans and drafts of Neuschwanstein. Elaborate carvings cover the beams and consoles of the ceiling.

Murals of the Tannhäuser saga by Josef Aigner: The itinerant knight and singer Tannhäuser falls in love with Elisabeth, niece of the Landgrave of Thüringen. Since the differences in their so-

cial status prevent them from ever marrying, he travels on in despair (»Tannhäuser playing for dancers«). Heedless of the warnings he receives, he enters the Hörselberg where the goddess Venus resides and for a year enjoys the pleasures of her realm (»Tannhäuser is warned by the faithful Eckhart« ■ »Tannhäuser in the Venus grotto«). However, he then grows weary of the goddess, leaves the Hörselberg and arrives once again at the Wartburg, where a Singers' Contest is taking place (»Shepherd boy playing a shawn in front of the Wartburg« ■ »Tannhäuser meets the Landgrave« ■ »Tannhäuser goes to the Wartburg« ■ Tannhäuser's arrival at the Wartburg ■ »Landgravine Elisabeth« ■ »Singers' Contest at the Wartburg«). Tannhäuser shocks the singers by singing in praise of sensual love. He is banned from the Wartburg, repents of his sins and goes on a pilgrimage to Rome to ask the Pope's forgiveness. This is refused him, and he returns to Venus' enchanted mountain (»Tannhäuser as a penitent before Pope Urban IV« ■ »Tannhäuser's return to Venus' enchanted mountain«). Mural of medieval rulers: »Duke Friedrich the Valiant of Austria« ■ »Duke Otto the Illustrious of Landshut«.

## 🔟 ANTEROOM

The oak-panelled anteroom or adjutant room is furnished with a table, chairs and a tiled stove, as well as a couch for the use of the servant waiting on the king at night. As in the study, the room is divided by two arches and pillars.

## 🔢 PASSAGE

## 🔢 UPPER HALL

From the upper hall on the fourth floor a marble portal on the west side leads to the gallery of the Throne Hall and two marble portals on the east side lead into the

Singers' Hall. The murals illustrate the Gudrun saga from the Old Norse Edda, the continuation of the Sigurd saga (see Room 1).

Murals of the Gudrun saga by Wilhelm Hauschild (1883/84): Gudrun corresponds to Kriemhild in the Nibelungen saga. After Sigurd's death she lives in solitude, but then marries Atli (Attila), king of the Huns (»Gudrun goes to reside with Thora after Sigurd's death« ■ »Gudrun embroidering the heroic deeds of her ancestors with Thora« ■ »Atli woos Gudrun« ■ »Gudrun's bridal journey with Atli«). In order to gain possession of the Nibelungen treasure, Atli invites Gudrun's brothers to his court. In the battle for the treasure, the Nibelungs are killed (»Atli tells Gudrun his dreams« ■ »Atli's messengers at the court of Gunnar« ■ »The battle between the Nibelungs and the Huns«). Gudrun

*Anteroom for the footman on duty, decorated more simply than the king's apartments*

»Gudrun greeting her brothers«, mural illustrating the Gudrun legend in the Upper Hall by Wilhelm Hauschild, 1883/84, ceiling painting and marble portal with Bavarian lion and swan coat of arms designed by Julius Hofmann

avenges them by stabbing Atli in his sleep and setting fire to the hall where the king's followers are sleeping. She tries to end her life by leaping into the sea but is borne on the waves to the coast of King Jonakur's realm. (»Gudrun holds a funeral repast for the warriors« ■ »Gunnar fettered in the castle tower« ■ »Gudrun throws the torch into the castle« ■ »Gudrun borne alive to distant shores«).

### 14 SINGERS' HALL

The Singers' Hall was one of the king's favourite projects and next to the Throne Hall the most important room in the castle. It occupies the whole of the fourth floor in the eastern section of the Palas and is a combination of two historical rooms in the Wartburg – the Festival Hall and the Singers' Hall. The Singers' Hall in the Wartburg was allegedly the location of the famous Singers' Contest which is also featured in Richard Wagner's opera »Tannhäuser«. In 1867 Ludwig II went at Wagner's suggestion to look at the Wartburg.

On the short, western side is the Singers' Bower, separated from the rest of the room by steps and three arcades, and with a small gallery above it. The murals in the hall do not however deal primarily with the Singers' Contest but with the saga of Parzival and the Holy Grail (see box). The bower, which resembles a stage, is painted with a forest scene – the sacred forest that surrounds the Castle of the Holy Grail. Parzival's son is the »Swan Knight« Lohengrin, with whom the picture cycle ends. Depicted on the high coffered ceiling are the signs of the zodiac.

Like the Throne Hall, this hall was also never used for large banquets or musical performances: it was Ludwig's monument to the knights and legends of medieval times. Tannhäuser, Parzival and Lohengrin were the figures with whom the king had identified since his youth.

Running along the long, north side is a gallery, with Flayetanis and Kyot, the authors or translators of the Grail saga, depicted on the consoles. Behind the retaining wall of the gallery is a passage with a coloured coffered ceiling painted with scrolls bearing the names of minnesingers. On the opposite, window wall, the ceiling consoles are carved with figures and symbols connected with the Parzival legend such as the winged Lucifer, who during his fall lost a precious stone from his crown, from which the Holy Grail was later made.

Murals of the Parzival saga in the hall by August Spieß (1883/84): On the window wall: »Parzival's first encounter with

*Following pages: Singers' Hall with Singers' Bower and gallery, murals illustrating the Parzival legend, chandeliers and candelabras of gilt brass*

# The Parzival saga

Queen Herzeloide brings up her son in isolation after the death of her consort Gamuret. However, after his first encounter with knights, he departs for the legendary court of King Arthur. Here Parzival meets the King of Cumberland, the »Red Knight«, whom he kills with his boy's spear. With the knight's armour he survives further adventures and he then marries Queen Kondwiramur. On

*»Parzival fighting the Red Knight«, mural in the Singers' Hall by August Spieß, 1883/84*

the way to visit his mother Parzival is received by the ailing king Amfortas at the Castle of the Holy Grail, Montsalvat, and at the banquet he sees the miraculous Grail. The knights hope that Parzival will release Amfortas from his suffering but Parzival fails to ask the king the crucial question about his health. That night Parzival is tortured by

nightmares and the following day he is scornfully dismissed from the castle. He roams restlessly from country to country; one Good Friday morning the hermit Trevrezent reveals to him the secret of the Grail. Continuing on his travels he encounters Gawan, the strongest of Arthur's knights, and defeats him without recognizing him. With the help of the sorceress Kundrie, Parzival finds his way back to the Castle of the Holy Grail, Montsalvat, where his wife Kondwiramur and their son Lohengrin are waiting for him. In Montsalvat he releases Amfortas by asking him sympathetically about his health and becomes King of the Holy Grail.

*Right: »Parzival at the court of Amfortas« (Castle of the Holy Grail), mural in the Singers' Hall by August Spieß, 1883/84*

*Castle kitchen with the latest technology of the day: a free-standing stove with an underground smoke outlet, a built-in oven, a sideboard and cupboards for keeping the food warm*

knighthood« ■ »Parzival taking leave of Herzeloide« ■ »Parzival's fight with the Red Knight« ■ »Parzival weds Kondwiramur« ■ »Parzival meets Amfortas«. In the quatrefoils above: »Repane and Feirefiz« ■ »Sigune and Schianatulander« ■ »Ginover and Artus« ■ »Herzeloide and Gamuret«. In the alcove: »Truth« ■ »Wisdom«. On the wall opposite the Singers' Bower: »Parzival at Amfortas' court« ■ »Parzival scorned by the castle guard« ■ »Parzival waited on by women« ■ »Parzival's dream«. On the gallery wall: »Kundrie summons Parzival« ■ »Parzival meets his half brother Feirefiz« ■ »Parzival visits the hermit Trevrezent« ■ »Kundrie's flight«. Above the entrance the royal Bavarian coat of arms: »Ludovicus II. rex.bavar.

com.palat.« (Ludwig II, King of Bavaria, Count Palatinate).
On the bower tondos with pictures of »Kardeiz« ■ »Lohengrin«
■ »Elsa« ■ »Prester John«, in the corner spandrels: »Parzival as
Grail King« ■ »Lohengrin leaves the Castle of the Holy Grail«.
On the side walls of the Bower: »Frau Minne« ■ »Walther von
der Vogelweide« ■ »Heinrich von Ofterdingen« ■ »Klingsor« ■
»Tree of Knowledge« ■ »Faith« ■ »Wolfram von Eschenbach«
■ »Scriber and Biterolf« ■ »Reimar von Zweter« ■ »The triumph
of faith«.

Murals of events leading up to the story of Parzival in the
gallery passage by August Spieß, Josef Munsch, Ferdinand Piloty and Waldemar Kolmsperger the Elder: »Gamuret in the
Moorish town of Patelamunt« ■ »Gamuret wins Herzeloid's
hand and crown« ■ »Constancy« ■ »Faithfulness« ■ »Gawan
bringing about the reconciliation and engagement of Melianze
and Obie« ■ »Gawan saves a wounded man« ■ »Temperance«.
■ In the oriel recess: »Justice« ■ »Fortitude«. On the window
wall: »Gawan's fight with the lion at Klingsor' enchanted
castle« ■ »Gawan breaks a branch from the tree of King Gra-
moflanz« ■ »Gawan and Orgeluse's wedding celebration« ■
»Gamuret's victory over Belakane's enemies« ■ »Bliss«. In the
anteroom: »Parzival meets pilgrims on Good Friday« (the king
ordered this picture to be completed on Good Friday 1884).

*Figure on p. 81:
King Ludwig II
of Bavaria in
general's
uniform and co-
ronation mantle.
Painting by
Ferdinand Piloty
the Younger,
1865, in the
King Ludwig II
Museum*

## KITCHEN

The kitchen was equipped with the latest technology of the
day. It included a large stove and a sideboard, a large and a
small spit, a built-in roasting oven with a plate warmer, a
baking oven, a mortar and a fish tank. Adjacent to it are the
pantry, with a built-in crockery cupboard and glass-parti-
tioned room for the chef-de-cuisine, and the scullery.

# Biographical data of King Ludwig II

His grandfather was King Ludwig I (reigned 1825–1848) who gave Munich a new status as a centre of the arts in Europe with monumental buildings and new collections. His son Maximilian II (reigned 1848–1864) married Princess Marie of Prussia, who was the mother of Ludwig II and Otto, in 1842.

**1845**  25 August: Ludwig II is born in Nymphenburg Palace near Munich, on the name day and birthday of his grandfather Ludwig I.

**1861**  2 February: Crown Prince Ludwig sees Richard Wagner's romantic opera »Lohengrin« for the first time.

**1864**  10 March: Death of Maximilian II; Ludwig II becomes king. 4 May: First meeting of the king with Richard Wagner.

**1865**  10 June: Premiere of »Tristan und Isolde« in the Munich Hof- and Nationaltheater.

**1866**  Bavaria loses the so-called »Bruderkrieg« against Prussia: from then on Ludwig II is no longer sovereign; this is a major catastrophe in his life and the main reason for his retreat from the realities of his position as a constitutional monarch.

**1867**  22 January: Engagement to Sophie, Duchess in Bavaria, sister of Empress Elisabeth of Austria.
31 May: Journey to the Wartburg, resulting in important ideas acquired for a new castle of his own.
20 July: Journey to Paris with his grandfather Ludwig I: visit to the World Exhibition in Paris and Versailles Palace.

*Royal House on the Schachen, exterior view
and Linderhof Palace (right side)*

He studies the palace with his Versailles project in mind and visits Pierrefonds Palace to obtain ideas for his new castle.
10 October: The engagement is broken off.

**1868**  21 June: Premiere of »Die Meistersinger von Nürnberg« in the Munich Hof- and Nationaltheater.
First drafts of Neuschwanstein Castle and the Versailles project.

**1869**  Drafts of a Byzantine palace and Linderhof Palace.
5 September: The foundation stone of Neuschwanstein is laid.
22 September: »Das Rheingold« by Richard Wagner is first performed in the Munich Hof- and Nationaltheater.

**1870** 26 June: Premiere of »Die Walküre« in the Munich Hof- and Nationaltheater.
Prussia's war with France: Bavaria is forced to fight on the side of Prussia.

**1871** Victory over France; the Prussian king becomes German emperor; Ludwig acknowledges him and in this way acquires certain

*The Great Hall of Mirrors in Herrenchiemsee Palace
and Herrenchiemsee Palace, exterior view (right side)*

independent rights for his subject state of Bavaria. From then on he concentrates on the development of his alternative world.

**1872**   6 May: First of a total of 209 »private shows«, theatre and opera performances for Ludwig II alone, most of them in the Hoftheater.
22 May: The foundation stone of the Festival Theatre in Bayreuth is laid.

**1873** Purchase of the Herreninsel in the Chiemsee.

**1874** Journey to Paris and Versailles; Ludwig studies the palace for his Versailles project.

**1876** 6–9 August and 27–31 August: Visit to the first Bayreuth Festival, dress rehearsal and third performance of »Der Ring des Nibelungen«.

**1878** 21 May: The foundation stone of the New Palace of Herrenchiemsee is laid.

**1879** Completion of Linderhof Palace.

*The new dress coach of King Ludwig II, 1870/71, Marstallmuseum in Nymphenburg Palace*

*King Ludwig II in civilian attire, photo by Joseph Albert, ca. 1885 (right side)*

**1883 to 1886**  Drafts of Falkenstein Castle, a Byzantine palace and a Chinese summer palace.
Increasing financial difficulties.

**1886**  10 June: Ludwig II is certified insane and his uncle Prince Luitpold of Bavaria takes over the regency for Ludwig's incurably ill younger brother.
12 June: Ludwig II is arrested in Neuschwanstein Castle and interned in Berg Palace on Lake Starnberg.
13 June: Ludwig II dies in Lake Starnberg, together with the psychiatrist who certified him insane.
19 June: King Ludwig II of Bavaria is laid to rest in the crypt of St Michael's Church in Munich.

# Index of artists and craftsmen

# Further Literature

W. RICHTER: Ludwig II., König von Bayern. München 11. Aufl. 1985 (1. Aufl. 1939).

H. KREISEL: Die Schlösser Ludwigs II. von Bayern. Darmstadt 1955.

D. and M. PETZET: Die Richard-Wagner-Bühne König Ludwigs II. München 1970.

R. HACKER: Ludwig II. von Bayern in Augenzeugenberichten. München 1972 ff.

S. RUSS: Die Ikonographie der Wandmalereien in Schloß Neuschwanstein. Diss. Heidelberg 1974.

J. TSCHOEKE: Neuschwanstein. Planungs- und Baugeschichte eines königlichen Burgbaus im ausgehenden 19. Jahrhundert. Diss. München 1975.

G. BAUMGARTNER: Königliche Träume. Ludwig II. und seine Bauten. München 1981.

H. G. EVERS: Ludwig II. Theaterfürst, König, Bauherr. München 1986.

E. HANSLIK und J. WAGNER: Ludwig II. König von Bayern (1845–1886). Internationale Bibliographie zu Leben und Wirkung. Frankfurt/Main 1986.

G. HOJER (Hg.): König Ludwig II.-Museum Herrenchiemsee. Katalog. München 1986.

L. HÜTTL: Ludwig II., König von Bayern. Eine Biographie. München 1986.

E. D. SCHMID: König Ludwig II. im Portrait. München 1996.

M. SPANGENBERG: Der Thronsaal von Schloß Neuschwanstein. König Ludwig II. und sein Verständnis vom Gottesgnadentum. Also available in English (The Throne Room in Schloss Neuschwanstein. Ludwig II of Bavaria and his vision of Divine Right). Regensburg 1999.

J. L. SCHLIM: Ludwig II. Traum und Technik. München 2001.

A. SCHICK: Möbel für den Märchenkönig. Ludwig II. und die Münchner Hofschreinerei Anton Pössenbacher. Furniture for the Dream King. Ludwig II and the Munich Court Cabinet-Maker Anton Pössenbacher (in German and English). Stuttgart 2003.

Picture book for children: P. O. KRÜCKMANN: Der König und sein Schloss Neuschwanstein. München 2001.

# Neuschwanstein Plans

3<sup>rd</sup> Floor

4<sup>th</sup> Floor

0  5  10  20  30 metres

**Ground plan of the complex**

- **a** Staircase Tower
- **b** Knights' House
- **c** Square Tower
- **d** Connecting Building
- **e** Hall
- **f** Entrance Hall
- **g** Palas
- **h** Upper Courtyard
- **i** Lower Courtyard
- **j** Gateway Building
- **k** Staircase Tower
- **l** Bower

**Palas 3rd Floor**

1. Lower Hall
2. Throne Hall
3. Anteroom
4. Dining Room
5. Bedroom
6. Oratory
7. Dressing Room
8. Salon
9. Grotto and Conservatory
10. Study
11. Anteroom (Adjutant's Room)
12. Passage

**Palas 4th Floor**

2. Throne Hall
13. Upper Hall
14. Singers' Hall

# PLACES OF INTEREST ADMINISTERED BY THE BAVARIAN PALACE DEPARTMENT
www.schloesser.bayern.de

**Ansbach** ■ **Residence of the Margraves of Ansbach**
Early rococo state apartments, collection of Ansbach faience and porcelain, Court Garden with orangery
**TEL.** (09 81) 95 38 39 - 0 · **FAX** (09 81) 95 38 39 - 40

**Aschaffenburg** ■ **Johannisburg Palace**
Art gallery and electoral apartments, collection of cork models, Palace Garden, Municipal Palace Museum
**TEL.** (0 60 21) 3 86 57 - 0 · **FAX** (0 60 21) 3 86 57 - 16

■ **Pompeiianum**
Replica of a Roman villa and Antiquities Museum

■ **Schönbusch Palace and Park**
Small neoclassical palace in an English landscape garden

**Bamberg** ■ **New Residence in Bamberg**
Imperial Hall and baroque state rooms, art gallery, Rose Garden
**TEL.** (09 51) 5 19 39 - 0 and 5 19 39 - 113
**FAX** (09 51) 5 19 39 - 1 29

**Bamberg/** ■ **Seehof Palace**
**Memmelsdorf** Residential and state rooms, rococo garden, cascade with waterworks
**TEL.** (09 51) 40 95 - 70 · **FAX** (09 51) 40 95 - 72

**Bayreuth** ■ **New Palace**
Margravial residence in the Bayreuth rococo style with the Wilhelmine Museum, the Museum of Bayreuth Faience, Court Garden with orangery
**TEL.** (09 21) 7 59 69 - 0 · **FAX** (09 21) 7 59 69 - 15

■ **Margravial Opera House**

**Bayreuth/** ■ **Museum of Garden Design Fantaisie Palace and Park**
**Donndorf** **TEL.** (09 21) 73 14 00 - 11 · **FAX** (09 21) 73 14 00 - 15

**Bayreuth/** ■ **Hermitage Old Palace**
**Hermitage** Margravine Wilhelmine's rooms, grotto, historic gardens with waterworks
**TEL.** (09 21) 7 59 69 - 37 · **FAX** (09 21) 7 59 69 - 41

**Bayreuth/ ■ Sanspareil**
**Wonsees**    Rock Garden and Oriental Building
          Rococo rooms, garden parterre and Rock Garden
          **TEL.** (0 92 74) 33-0 or 12 21

          **■ Zwernitz Castle** Castle complex

**Burghausen ■ Burghausen Castle**
          Castle complex, ducal apartments, chapel, State Gallery of Old
          German Masters and Historical Paintings, viewing platform
          **TEL.** (0 86 77) 46 59 · **FAX** (0 86 77) 6 56 74

**Cadolzburg ■ Cadolzburg Castle** Tel./FAX: see Nuremberg

**Coburg ■ Ehrenburg Palace**
          Historical residential and state rooms from the baroque era and
          the 19th century
          **TEL.** (0 95 61) 80 88-0 · **FAX** (0 95 61) 80 88-40

**Coburg/ ■ Rosenau Palace**
**Rödental**    Set in an English landscape garden; residential rooms from the
          Biedermeier period and neo-Gothic Marble Hall
          **TEL.** (0 95 63) 30 84-0 · **FAX** (0 95 61) 30 84-29

**Dachau ■ Dachau Palace**
          Hall, staircase, Court Garden
          **TEL.** (0 81 31) 8 79 23 · **FAX** (0 81 31) 7 85 73

**Eichstätt ■ Willibaldsburg**
          Fortress complex, Jura Museum, Prehistoric and Early History
          Museum, Bastion Garden
          **TEL.** (0 84 21) 47 30 · **FAX** (0 84 21) 81 94

**Ellingen ■ Ellingen Residence**
          The state apartments of Prince von Wrede, rooms of the
          Deutscher Orden, palace church, historical park
          **TEL.** (0 91 41) 9 74 79-0 · **FAX** (0 91 41) 9 74 79-7

**Feldafing ■ Feldafing Park and Rose Island**
**Lake Starnberg    TEL.** (0 81 51) 69 75 · **FAX** (0 81 51) 36 81 23

**Herrenchiemsee ■ Herrenchiemsee New Palace**
          Residential and state rooms, historical gardens with waterworks
          and King Ludwig II Museum
          **TEL.** (0 80 51) 68 87-0 · **FAX** (0 80 51) 68 87-99

          **■ Museum in the Augustinian monastery Herrenchiemsee (Old Palac**
          Permanent exhibition on the former monastery and the constitutional

conference, apartment of King Ludwig II;
Julius Exter Art Gallery; Maler am Chiemsee Gallery

**Höchstädt** ■ **Höchstädt Palace**
Exhibition on the Battle of Höchstädt/Blenheim 1704,
Chapel, collection of faience from southwest Germany
**TEL.** (0 90 74) 9 58 57 12 · **FAX** (0 90 74) 9 58 57 91

**Holzhausen** ■ **Gasteiger House**
Collection of Anna and Mathias Gasteiger's works in the rooms of
the summer villa where they lived, landscape garden
**TEL.** (0 88 06) 26 82

**Kelheim** ■ **Hall of Liberation**
Neoclassical memorial, impressive domed hall, view of the
surroundings from the open gallery
**TEL.** (0 94 41) 6 82 07-0 · **FAX** (0 94 41) 6 82 07-7

**Kempten** ■ **Kempten Residence**
State rooms and Throne Room of the prince-abbots
**TEL.** (08 31) 2 56 - 2 51 · **FAX** (08 31) 2 56 - 2 60

**Königssee** ■ **St Bartholomä**
Church St. Bartholomä, hunting lodge, chapel of St Johann and
St Paul, Berchtesgaden national park
**TEL.** (0 80 51) 9 66 58 - 0 · **FAX** (0 80 51) 9 66 58 - 38

**Kulmbach** ■ **Plassenburg**
Schöner Hof (Beautiful Courtyard), Hohenzollern Museum,
»Frederick the Great« Army Museum
**TEL.** (0 92 21) 82 20 - 0 · **FAX** (0 92 21) 82 20 - 26

**Landshut** ■ **Trausnitz Castle**
Castle complex, medieval halls and castle chapel, Fools' Staircase,
Renaissance rooms, Museum of Renaissance Art
**TEL.** (08 71) 9 24 11 - 0/- 44 · **FAX** (08 71) 9 24 11 - 40

■ **Town Residence**
Arcaded courtyard, Italian Renaissance halls, chapel, neoclassical
Birkenfeld Rooms

**Lauenstein** ■ **Lauenstein Castle**
**near Ludwigsstadt** Castle complex, residential rooms, special museum collections
**TEL.** (0 92 63) 4 00 · **FAX** (0 92 63) 97 44 22

**Linderhof** ■ **Linderhof Palace**
Residential and state rooms, Venus Grotto, Moroccan House,

Moorish Kiosk, Hunding's Hut and the Hermitage of Gurnemanz, historic gardens with waterworks
**TEL.** (0 88 22) 92 03 - 0 · **FAX** (0 88 22) 92 03 - 11

**Munich** ■ **Munich Residence and Court Garden**
Historical residential and state rooms representing a range of epochs from the Renaissance to the 19th century, court church and chapel, special collections (silver, porcelain, sacred vestments, reliquaries)
**TEL.** (0 89) 2 90 67 - 1 · **FAX** (0 89) 2 90 67 - 2 25

**Treasury of the Residence**

**Cuvilliés Theatre**

■ **Feldherrnhalle (Field Marshals' Hall)**

■ **Hall of Fame and statue of Bavaria** on the Theresienhöhe

■ **Nymphenburg Palace**
State rooms, Great Hall, Gallery of Beauties, palace chapel
**TEL.** (0 89) 1 79 08 - 0 · **FAX** (0 89) 1 79 08 - 6 27

**Amalienburg, Badenburg, Pagodenburg, Magdalenenklause**
in the historical palace park

**Marstallmuseum**
Court carriages and sleighs, saddles and other riding equipment

**Museum of Nymphenburg Porcelain** Bäuml Collection

■ **English Garden** Landscape garden in the English style
**TEL.** (0 89) 3 86 66 39 - 0 · **FAX** (0 89) 3 86 66 39 - 23

**Munich/** ■ **Schleißheim New Palace**
**Oberschleißheim** Halls, state apartments, art gallery, baroque Court Garden
**TEL.** (0 89) 31 58 72 - 0 · **FAX** (0 89) 31 58 72 - 50

■ **Lustheim Palace** Museum of Meißen Porcelain, hall

**Neuburg** ■ **Neuburg Palace on the Danube**
**a.d. Donau** Sgraffito façade, 1st Protestant chapel, grottoes, Pfalz-Neuburg and Baroque Church Museum, Museum of Archaeology, State Gallery of Flemish Art
**TEL.** (0 84 31) 64 43 - 0 · **FAX** (0 84 31) 64 43 - 44

**Neuschwan-** ■ **Neuschwanstein Castle**
**stein/** Royal apartments and state rooms
**Schwangau** **TEL.** (0 83 62) 9 39 88 - 0 · **FAX** (0 83 62) 9 39 88 - 18

**Nuremberg** ■ **Imperial Castle of Nuremberg**
Palas, period rooms, double chapel, Deep Well and Sinwell Tower,
Castle Gardens
**TEL.** (09 11) 24 46 59 - 0 · **FAX** (09 11) 24 46 59 - 300

**Prunn** ■ **Prunn Castle**
**im Altmühltal** Historical castle rooms, chapel
**TEL.** (0 94 42) 33 23 · **FAX** (0 94 42) 33 35

**Riedenburg** ■ **Rosenburg Castle**
Castle complex with a privately run falconry
**TEL.** (0 94 42) 27 52 · **FAX** (0 94 42) 33 35

**Schachen** ■ **King's House on the Schachen**
Residential rooms and Turkish Hall, alpine garden
**TEL.** (01 72) 8 76 88 68 and (0 88 22) 92 03 - 0
**FAX** (0 88 22) 92 03 - 11

**Schnaittach** ■ **Rothenburg Fortress**
The ruins of an 18th-century fortress complex
**TEL.** (0 91 53) 77 93

**Übersee/** ■ **Exter House**
**Feldwies** With the atelier of the artist Julius Exter
**TEL.** (0 86 42) 89 50 - 83 · **FAX** (0 86 42) 89 50 - 85

**Veitshöchheim** ■ **Veitshöchheim Palace and Garden**
Historical residential rooms,
Exhibition on the history of the Court Garden,
Rococo Garden with waterworks
**TEL.** (09 31) 9 15 82

**Wonsees** ■ **See Bayreuth**

**Würzburg** ■ **Würzburg Residence**
Baroque state rooms, frescos by G.B. Tiepolo, art gallery,
Court Gardens
**TEL.** (09 31) 3 55 17 - 0 · **FAX** (09 31) 3 55 17 - 25

■ **Marienburg Fortress**
Fortress complex, Prince's Building Museum with Treasury,
Sacred Vestment Room and municipal history collections,
Maschikuli Tower, Prince's Garden, Main-Franconian Museum

# THE PUBLICATIONS OF THE BAVARIAN PALACE DEPARTMENT

The Bavarian Palace Department publishes official guides with colour photos on all the places of interest for which it is responsible; a number of these are available in several languages. It also offers plans of many of the parks accompanied by brief, illustrated descriptions. Exhibition catalogues and inventories, picture books and scientific works complete the varied spectrum of publications. In addition to the books there are also posters, CD-ROMs and videos on individual properties and special topics.

A complete list of publications can be ordered free of charge from the following address:

 Bayerische Verwaltung der
staatlichen Schlösser, Gärten und Seen

Postfach 20 20 63 · 80020 München
Tel. (0 89) 1 79 08-0 · Fax (0 89) 1 79 08-190
online-bookshop: www.schloesser.bayern.de

# OFFICIAL GUIDES

Published in German; some also available in English, French, Italian, Spanish and Japanese

| | |
|---|---|
| Ansbach | Residenz Ansbach |
| Aschaffenburg | Aschaffenburg Castle and Pompeiianum; Schloss und Park Schönbusch |
| Bamberg/Memmelsdorf | Neue Residenz Bamberg (with English summary); Seehof Palace and Park |
| Bayreuth | The Hermitage at Bayreuth; Margravial Opera House Bayreuth (with English summary), Neues Schloss Bayreuth |
| Bayreuth/Wonsees | Felsengarten Sanspareil; Burg Zwernitz (with English summary) |
| Burghausen | Burg zu Burghausen (with English summary) |
| Coburg | Coburg Ehrenburg Palace |
| Coburg/Rödental | Schloss Rosenau (with English summary) |
| Dachau | Schloss Dachau |
| Eichstätt | Willibaldsburg Eichstätt |
| Ellingen | Residenz Ellingen |
| Feldafing | Die Roseninsel im Starnberger See |
| Herrenchiemsee | Augustinian Monastery and New Palace of Herrenchiemsee |
| Kelheim | Kelheim Hall of Liberation |
| Königsee | St. Bartholomä am Königssee (with English summary) |
| Kulmbach | Plassenburg ob Kulmbach |
| Landshut | Landshut Burg Trausnitz; Stadtresidenz Landshut |
| Lauenstein b. Ludwigsstadt | Burg Lauenstein |
| Linderhof | Linderhof Palace |
| Munich | Residence Munich; The Treasury in the Munich Residence; Altes Residenztheater/Cuvilliés-Theater; Englischer Garten München (with English summary); Ruhmeshalle und Bavaria; Nymphenburg, main palace, park and pavilions; Marstallmuseum Schloss Nymphenburg |
| Neuburg a.d. Donau | Schloss Neuburg a.d. Donau (with English summary) |
| Neuschwanstein | Neuschwanstein Castle |
| Nuremberg | Imperial Castle Nuremberg |
| Oberschleißheim | Schloss Schleißheim, Neues Schloss und Garten (with English summary) |
| Prunn | Burg Prunn |
| Riedenburg | Burg Rosenburg in Riedenburg an der Altmühl |
| Schachen | The Royal House on the Schachen |
| Veitshöchheim | Schloss Veitshöchheim und Hofgarten |
| Würzburg | Festung Marienberg zu Würzburg; The Würzburg Residence and Court Gardens |

The present edition of the Official Guide to Neuschwanstein was revised by Uwe Gerd Schatz and Friederike Ulrichs. It is based on the 1933 edition of the Neuschwanstein Official Guide, written by Heinrich Kreisel, expanded by Hans Thoma and subsequently revised by Michael Petzet, Gerhard Hojer and Horst Stierhof, with further revision by Elmar D. Schmid in 1991.

Picture credits: Bayerisches Hauptstaatsarchiv, Abteilung 3, Geheimes Hausarchiv, Kabinettsakten König Maximilian II. 12 p.: p. 8–9 • Josef Beck, Eschenlohe: cover • Diderot Verlag, Rottenburg: p. 76 • Kienberger, Lechbruck: p. 48, 72 • Metz, Tübingen: p. 47, 52–53, 68 • Nationalarchiv der Richard-Wagner-Stiftung, Bayreuth: p. 12 • Neumeister, München: p. 54 • Schöning & Co., Lübeck: p. 24–25, 44–45, 60, 78 • Wartburg-Stiftung, Eisenach: p. 33
All others: Bayerische Schlösserverwaltung/Rainer Herrmann/Ulrich Pfeuffer/Maria Scherf etc

Index of artists and craftsmen: Irmgard Killing

2nd edition of the new version
© Bayerische Verwaltung der staatlichen Schlösser, Gärten und Seen, München 2007
Project manager: Kathrin Jung
Translated by Sue Bollans
Edited by Irmgard Killing
Graphic design: Verena Fleischmann, Munich
Lithography: Reproline Genceller, Munich
Printed by Sellier Druck GmbH, Freising
ISBN 978-3-932982-85-9
Printed in Germany